DAN MCFARLAND

Using AI in the Classroom

First edition

This book was professionally typeset on Reedsy.
Find out more at reedsy.com

Contents

1

Chapter 1

Technology is transforming the way we live and work, and nowhere is this more evident than in the field of education. From online learning platforms to virtual reality simulations, technology is enabling new forms of learning and teaching that were once unimaginable. And at the forefront of this transformation is Artificial Intelligence (AI), a field that is rapidly advancing and revolutionizing many industries, including education.

In this book, we'll explore the power of AI in education, and how it is changing the way we teach and learn. We'll start by defining what AI is and how it works, and then move on to discuss the different types of AI and their applications in education. Finally, we'll examine some of the challenges and opportunities that AI presents for educators, and how we can best prepare for the future of education in the age of AI.

What is AI?

At its core, AI refers to computer systems designed to perform tasks normally requiring human intelligence. These tasks might include recognizing speech, interpreting images, or making decisions based on data. AI is based on a combination of computer science, mathematics, and cognitive science, and it is constantly evolving as new technologies and approaches are developed.

One of the key features of AI is its ability to learn and adapt based on experience. This is known as machine learning, and it involves training computer algorithms on large sets of data in order to identify patterns and make predictions. Machine learning is the foundation of many of the most powerful AI applications, including language models like GPT-3, which are capable of generating high-quality responses to a wide range of queries.

Types of AI and Their Applications in Education

There are several types of AI, each with its own strengths and weaknesses. Some of the most common types include rule-based models, statistical models, and neural network models. These models can be used in a variety of applications in education, including:

- Research: AI language models can be used to generate responses to research queries, making it easier and faster for teachers to find the information they need.
- Classroom Instruction: AI language models can be used to assist with classroom instruction by generating responses to student queries or providing feedback on student writing.
- Professional Development: AI language models can provide teachers personalized professional development resources based on their specific needs and interests.

Challenges and Opportunities for Educators

While AI presents many exciting opportunities for educators, it also poses several challenges. One of the biggest challenges is ensuring that AI is used in an ethical and responsible way, and that it does not perpetuate biases or reinforce inequalities. Additionally, there is a need for educators to develop new skills and knowledge in order to effectively use AI in their teaching practice.

Despite these challenges, AI presents a tremendous opportunity for educators to enhance teaching and learning in a variety of ways. By understanding the strengths and limitations of AI, and by staying up-to-date on the latest developments and best practices, educators can prepare themselves and their students for the future of education in the age of AI.

2

Chapter 2

As we explored in Chapter 1, AI has the potential to transform education in many ways, including research, assessment, and personalized learning. One of the most promising applications of AI in education is assisting with research and answering student queries. In this chapter, we will dive deeper into the art of writing effective queries for AI, and how to get the most out of this powerful tool.

What is a Query?

A query is a request for information, usually in the form of a question. In the context of AI, a query is typically entered into a computer system, which then uses machine learning algorithms to generate a response based on the data it has been trained on. The quality of the response depends on various factors, including the quality of the data, the complexity of the query, and the sophistication of the AI system.

Writing Effective Queries

Writing an effective query for an AI system is an art and a science. Here are some tips to keep in mind when crafting your queries:

1. Be Specific: The more specific your query is, the more likely you are to get a useful response. Avoid vague or open-ended queries, and try to be as precise as possible in your wording.

2. Use Natural Language: Many AI systems are designed to understand

natural language, so try to phrase your query in a way that sounds natural and conversational.

3. Provide Context: When asking a question, provide as much context as possible. This can help the AI system understand the meaning behind your query and generate a more accurate response.

4. Use Simple Language: Avoid using overly technical or complex language in your queries. Stick to simple, clear language that the AI system is more likely to understand.

5. Be Patient: AI systems can take some time to generate a response, especially if the query is complex or the data is large. Be patient and give the system time to do its work.

Examples of Effective Queries in Education

Let's look at some examples of effective queries in education. These examples illustrate how queries can be used to enhance teaching and learning in a variety of ways:

Research Query: "What are the latest studies on the effectiveness of project-based learning for middle school students?"

This query is specific and provides context, and is designed to help educators stay up to date with the latest research on project-based learning. By using AI to generate a response to this query, educators can save time and stay informed about the latest research findings.

Classroom Instruction Query: "What are some strategies for teaching multiplication to struggling third-grade students?"

This query is specific, uses natural language, and provides context by specifying the target audience of struggling third-grade students. By using AI to generate a response to this query, educators can get ideas for effective strategies to use in their classroom instruction.

Professional Development Query: "What are some effective strategies for using technology to teach writing in the high school English classroom?"

This query is specific and provides context, and is designed to help educators improve their use of technology in the classroom. By using AI to generate a response to this query, educators can learn about effective strategies for integrating technology into their writing instruction.

Student Query: "What is the Pythagorean theorem?"

This query is simple and straightforward, and is an example of how AI can be used to provide students with quick and accurate answers to their questions. By using AI to generate a response to this query, educators can provide students with instant feedback and support, helping to improve their learning outcomes.

Data Analysis Query: "What are the trends in student performance on the state math test over the past five years?"

This query is specific and provides context, and is an example of how AI can be used to assist with data analysis. By generating a response to this query, educators can quickly identify trends and patterns in student performance, which can help inform instructional decisions and improve learning outcomes.

Best Practices for Using AI in Education

In addition to writing effective queries, there are several best practices to keep in mind when using AI in education:

1. Use High-Quality Data: The quality of the data that AI systems are trained on has a direct impact on the quality of the responses they generate. Make sure the data you use is high-quality and relevant to your specific educational context.
2. Maintain Ethical Considerations: AI systems can be used to collect and analyze sensitive data about students and educators. It is important to maintain ethical considerations when using AI, and to ensure that data is collected and used in an ethical and responsible way.
3. Evaluate Responses: It is important to evaluate the responses generated by AI systems to ensure that they are accurate and useful. This may

involve comparing AI-generated responses to responses generated by human experts, or conducting follow-up research to verify the accuracy of the responses.

4. Continuously Improve: AI systems are constantly evolving, and it is important to stay up to date with the latest developments and best practices in AI. This may involve ongoing training and professional development for educators, as well as regular evaluations of AI systems to ensure that they are meeting the needs of educators and students.

Chapter 3

As AI technology continues to evolve, educators are increasingly looking to these tools as a way to transform teaching and learning. In this chapter, we will explore some specific use cases for AI in education and examine how these tools are being used to improve learning outcomes.

Personalized Learning

One of the most promising use cases for AI in education is personalized learning. Traditional classroom instruction often relies on a one-size-fits-all approach, which can leave some students behind while others are bored or disengaged. AI tools, such as intelligent tutoring systems, can be used to provide personalized instruction and feedback to students, based on their individual learning needs and preferences.

Intelligent tutoring systems use algorithms to analyze student data, such as their responses to practice problems, and then provide tailored instruction and feedback based on their learning needs. For example, if a student struggles with a particular concept, the system can offer additional practice problems or provide additional explanations until the student has demonstrated mastery.

By providing personalized instruction, educators can help to improve learning outcomes and enhance student engagement. Moreover, AI tools can help to reduce the workload of educators by automating some aspects of instruction, such as grading and feedback.

Adaptive Testing

Another use case for AI in education is adaptive testing. Adaptive testing uses machine learning algorithms to dynamically adjust the difficulty of test questions based on a student's responses. This approach can help to reduce testing time and improve test accuracy, as well as provide more accurate assessments of student learning.

Adaptive testing is particularly useful for evaluating student mastery of complex skills and knowledge areas. For example, a math test could dynamically adjust the difficulty of questions based on a student's responses to ensure that they are being challenged appropriately.

AI tools can also be used to provide feedback on test performance, such as highlighting areas where a student may need additional practice. Moreover, AI tools can help to reduce the workload of educators by automating some aspects of test administration and grading.

Automated Grading and Feedback

Automated grading and feedback is another way that educators are using AI to transform teaching and learning. Automated grading and feedback systems can analyze student work and provide instant feedback on errors and areas for improvement. This approach can help to improve the quality and speed of grading, as well as provide more timely and effective feedback to students.

Automated grading and feedback systems can be used for a variety of assignments, including essays, math problems, and programming assign-ments. These systems use natural language processing and machine learning algorithms to analyze student work and provide feedback that is specific and targeted.

AI-powered grading and feedback can help to reduce the workload of educators, allowing them to focus on other aspects of instruction, such as lesson planning and student support. Additionally, AI tools can provide more consistent and objective feedback, reducing the potential for grading bias.

Language Learning

AI can also be used to enhance language learning in a variety of ways. For example, natural language processing tools can be used to analyze and provide feedback on student writing, or to provide real-time translation services for students who speak languages other than English. AI-powered chat bots and virtual assistants can also be used to provide students with language practice and support outside of regular class hours.

AI tools can also be used to create personalized language learning plans that are tailored to the individual needs and preferences of each student. For example, a language learning app could use machine learning algorithms to analyze a student's language abilities and provide practice exercises that are challenging but not too difficult.

Predictive Analytics

Finally, predictive analytics is another use case for AI in education that has the potential to transform teaching and learning. Predictive analytics can be used to identify at-risk students early, and to provide targeted interventions to prevent academic difficulties. Predictive analytics can also be used to identify patterns in student data, such as attendance or engagement, that may indicate a need for additional support.

By analyzing student data, AI tools can help educators identify which students are most likely to struggle with specific topics or skills, and then provide targeted support to help these students succeed. For example, if a student consistently performs poorly on math quizzes, an AI tool could provide additional practice exercises or recommend a one-on-one tutoring session with a math teacher.

Additionally, predictive analytics can be used to identify trends and patterns in student data that may indicate broader issues with curriculum or instruction. For example, if multiple students consistently struggle with a particular concept, an AI tool could help educators identify the root cause of this issue and make adjustments to the curriculum or instructional methods to better support student learning.

Overall, predictive analytics has the potential to help educators make data-driven decisions that lead to improved learning outcomes for all students.

4

Chapter 4

As AI technology continues to advance, it is increasingly being used in education to assist with tasks such as assessment, personalized learning, and administrative tasks. While AI has the potential to enhance education, it is important to consider the ethical implications of using this technology. In this chapter, we will explore some of the key ethical considerations surrounding the use of AI in education and discuss best practices for ensuring that AI is used in a responsible and ethical manner.

Transparency and Explainability

Transparency and explainability are key ethical considerations when it comes to using AI in education. The algorithms and models used by AI tools must be transparent and explainable so that students, parents, and educators can understand how decisions are being made. This is particularly important for sensitive areas such as assessment and grading, where students have a right to understand how their work is being evaluated.

To promote transparency and explainability, educators and administrators should consider implementing measures such as providing students with access to their own data, providing detailed explanations of how AI tools are being used, and allowing for human oversight to ensure that decisions made by AI tools are fair and unbiased.

Data Privacy and Security

Data privacy and security is another key ethical consideration when it comes to using AI in education. As AI tools collect and analyze large amounts of student data, it is critical that this data is protected and used only for its intended purposes. Educators and administrators must ensure that student data is collected and stored in compliance with applicable privacy laws and that appropriate safeguards are in place to prevent unauthorized access or use.

To promote data privacy and security, educators and administrators should consider implementing measures such as using secure data storage and transmission methods, limiting access to student data to authorized personnel, and ensuring that third-party vendors used for AI tools comply with applicable privacy laws and standards.

Bias and Discrimination

Bias and discrimination are major ethical considerations when it comes to using AI in education. AI tools are only as unbiased as the data on which they are trained, and there is a risk that AI tools may perpetuate or even amplify existing biases in education.

To address this concern, educators and administrators must take steps to ensure that AI tools are designed and trained in a way that minimizes bias and discrimination. This may involve using diverse data sets for training, testing AI tools for bias and discrimination, and establishing ethical guidelines or standards for the use of AI in education that prioritize fairness and equity.

In addition, educators and administrators must be vigilant for unintended consequences of using AI in education. For example, there is a risk that AI tools may reinforce or exacerbate existing achievement gaps between different student groups, or that the use of AI tools may displace or devalue the role of educators in the classroom.

Ethical Decision-Making

When using AI in education, it is important to engage in ethical decision-making to ensure that the technology is used in a responsible and ethical manner. This involves considering the potential impact of AI on students, assessing the risks and benefits of using AI tools, and ensuring that ethical principles such as fairness, equity, and respect for student privacy are upheld.

To facilitate ethical decision-making, educators and administrators should consider establishing ethical guidelines or standards for the use of AI in education, providing training on ethical considerations related to AI, and involving diverse stakeholders such as students, parents, and educators in decision-making processes related to the use of AI.

5

Chapter 5

Artificial intelligence has the potential to revolutionize the field of education by providing new tools and methods for teaching and learning. In this chapter, we will delve into the ways in which AI is currently being used in education, the benefits and challenges of using AI in the classroom, and how educators can effectively integrate AI into their teaching practices.

Current Applications of AI in Education

AI is being used in education in a variety of ways, including:

- Adaptive learning: AI algorithms can analyze data on student performance and tailor learning experiences to individual students based on their strengths, weaknesses, and learning styles. This allows for a more personalized and effective learning experience for students.
- Intelligent tutoring systems: These AI systems provide students with personalized feedback, guidance, and support as they work through learning activities and assessments. They can also track student progress and provide teachers with data to inform their teaching.
- Automated grading and assessment: AI can analyze student work and provide automated grading and feedback, freeing up teachers' time and providing students with instant feedback. This allows for faster and more

accurate grading.

· Language learning: AI-powered chat bots and language learning platforms can provide interactive and personalized language learning experiences, allowing students to practice their language skills in a more engaging way.

· Educational research: AI can be used to analyze large datasets and identify patterns and insights that can inform educational research and practice. This can lead to more effective teaching strategies and better student outcomes.

Benefits of Using AI in Education

Using AI in education can offer a number of benefits, including:

· Personalized learning experiences that meet the needs of individual students. AI algorithms can tailor learning experiences to each student's strengths, weaknesses, and learning style, providing a more effective and engaging learning experience.

· Increased efficiency and productivity, as AI can automate time-consuming tasks such as grading and assessment. This allows teachers to spend more time on teaching and interacting with their students.

· Improved student engagement and motivation through interactive and personalized learning experiences. AI-powered tools can make learning more interactive and engaging, leading to increased student motivation and interest in the material.

· Enhanced data analysis and insights, providing teachers with more accurate and detailed information about student performance. This allows for more effective teaching strategies and interventions.

· Access to educational opportunities and resources for students who may not have had them otherwise. AI-powered tools can provide access to educational opportunities and resources that might otherwise be unavailable to students, regardless of their location or socioeconomic status.

Challenges of Using AI in Education

While the potential benefits of using AI in education are significant, there are also several challenges that need to be considered, including:

- Ethical and privacy concerns related to collecting and using student data. AI systems collect a lot of data on students, and it is important to ensure that this data is being collected and used in an ethical and responsible way.
- The potential for AI systems to perpetuate existing biases and inequalities in education. If AI algorithms are not carefully designed and tested, they can perpetuate existing biases and inequalities in education, leading to unfair outcomes for certain groups of students.
- The need for teachers to have the skills and knowledge to effectively integrate AI into their teaching practices. Teachers need to have the necessary skills and knowledge to use AI effectively in the classroom, and this may require additional training and professional development.
- The risk of relying too heavily on technology and neglecting the importance of human interaction and engagement in the learning process. While AI can enhance the learning experience, it is important to remember that human interaction and engagement are still crucial for effective teaching and learning.

How Educators Can Integrate AI into Their Teaching Practices

To effectively integrate AI into their teaching practices, educators should:

Understand the different types of AI applications available and their potential benefits and limitations. In addition, AI can also help teachers to personalize the learning experience for each student. With the help of AI-powered tools, teachers can better understand their students' strengths and weaknesses, learning style, and pace. This information can be used to create customized lesson plans and assignments that cater to each student's individual needs. AI can also provide real-time feedback to students, helping them to identify areas where they need to improve and offering personalized recommendations for further study.

Moreover, AI can help teachers to evaluate the effectiveness of their teaching methods and make data-driven decisions to improve student outcomes. By analyzing student performance data, AI can identify which teaching strategies are most effective and which need to be adjusted. This can help teachers to optimize their teaching approach and ensure that students are getting the most out of their education.

Another area where AI can be beneficial in education is in the detection of student mental health issues. AI-powered tools can analyze student behavior patterns, social media activity, and other data sources to detect signs of anxiety, depression, or other mental health issues. This can help teachers to identify at-risk students and provide them with the support and resources they need to succeed academically and personally.

Finally, AI can help to improve school safety by analyzing surveillance footage and detecting potential threats. With the help of AI-powered tools, schools can identify suspicious behavior and alert authorities to potential dangers before they escalate.

6

Chapter 6

Artificial Intelligence (AI) has the potential to transform education by enabling personalized learning, automating administrative tasks, and providing new opportunities for students and teachers. However, as with any technology, the use of AI in education raises ethical concerns and requires responsible use. This chapter will discuss some of the ethical considerations and best practices for using AI in education.

Ethical considerations in AI education

One of the most significant ethical concerns surrounding AI in education is the potential for bias. AI systems can perpetuate existing biases, such as those based on race, gender, or socioeconomic status. For example, an AI-powered grading system may be biased against students from certain racial or socioeconomic backgrounds if the system was trained on data that over-represents those groups.

Another ethical consideration is data privacy. AI in education relies on vast amounts of student data, such as grades, attendance records, and behavioral data. This data is sensitive and should be protected from unauthorized access, use, or disclosure. Institutions using AI should be transparent about how student data is being collected, used, and protected.

Best practices for using AI in education

To ensure responsible use of AI in education, institutions should adhere to some best practices:

1. Foster transparency and accountability: Institutions should be transparent about how they are using AI in education and be accountable for the outcomes. Teachers and students should be aware of how AI is being used in the classroom and have access to information about how the system works.

2. Prioritize data privacy: Institutions should prioritize data privacy and implement robust security measures to protect student data. This includes obtaining consent from students and parents/guardians, minimizing the collection and retention of data, and using secure storage and transmission methods.

3. Ensure fairness and non-discrimination: Institutions should strive to ensure that their AI systems do not perpetuate biases or discriminate against any group of students.

4. Provide human oversight: Institutions should provide human oversight and intervention in AI systems to ensure that they are working as intended and not causing harm.

5. Evaluate the effectiveness of AI in education: Institutions should evaluate the effectiveness of AI in education regularly. This includes examining the impact on student outcomes, identifying areas for improvement, and ensuring that the benefits outweigh the risks.

One of the main challenges of implementing AI in the classroom is getting started. Here are some practical steps that educators can take to integrate AI into their teaching practice:

1. Start with a clear goal: Before introducing AI, it's essential to identify a clear goal that aligns with your teaching philosophy and the learning outcomes you want to achieve. By setting specific goals, you can evaluate whether AI is the best tool to achieve your objectives.

2. Identify potential use cases: Once you have a clear goal in mind, it's time

to identify potential use cases for AI in your classroom. For example, you could use AI-powered chat bots to answer student questions or use AI algorithms to personalize learning experiences based on student performance.

3. Choose the right tools: There are many different AI tools and platforms available, so it's crucial to choose the right one for your needs. Consider factors like ease of use, cost, and compatibility with your existing technology stack.

4. Involve students in the process: AI is a complex topic, and involving students in the process of implementing AI in the classroom can help them understand how it works and the benefits it provides. Encourage students to experiment with AI tools and provide feedback on their experiences.

5. Start small: Implementing AI can be overwhelming, so it's essential to start small and gradually build up your capabilities over time. For example, you could start by introducing a simple chat bot to answer student questions before moving on to more advanced use cases.

6. Leverage existing resources: There are many resources available to educators who want to integrate AI into their teaching practice, including online courses, tutorials, and communities. Take advantage of these resources to learn more about AI and how it can be used in the classroom.

By following these steps, educators can begin to leverage the power of AI to create more personalized and engaging learning experiences for their students.